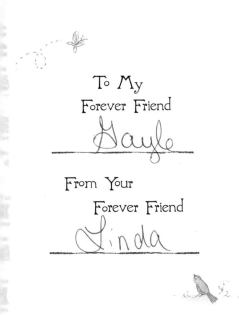

To My
Forever Friend

Gayle

From Your
Forever Friend

Linda

Forever Friends

Illustrated by Becky Kelly
Written by Patrick Regan

Andrews McMeel Publishing

Kansas City

Forever Friends

illustrations copyright © 2002 by Becky Kelly;
text copyright © 2002 by Patrick Regan.

For information, write
Andrews McMeel Publishing,
4520 Main Street,
Kansas City, Missouri 64111.

www.andrewsmcmeel.com
www.beckykelly.com

10 9 8 7

ISBN: 0-7407-2355-3

Edited by Jean Lowe
Designed by Stephanie Farley
Production by Elizabeth Nuelle

Forever Friends

I've been thinking

about you and me

And how our friendship

came to be—

—how long ago
I hoped that we—

could be forever friends.

And now I look back
on those days

And smile at

all the little ways—

—we made the
tough times
seem okay

Like true forever friends.

At times we'd laugh
so hard
and then,

We'd catch our breath

and   again

start

'Cause having fun

comes easy when

You're with
forever friends.

Together we've shared
wondrous
sights

Like soft
        spring days

and starlit nights

When all the world
seems still and right

With my forever friend.

And on those days
when
rain
would
fall

And life
was not
much fun
at all

You were always there
to take my call,

A true forever friend.

Life's winding roads
may take us far

But if we're apart,
let each
bright star

Remind us just how
blessed we are

To be forever friends.

And when the stars
           shine down,
     we'll see

Perhaps by fate
or destiny—

A friendship that
was meant to be—

You and me—